THIS BOOK is to
commemorate the issuance of the
Chickasaw medal
January 1, 1974
and is limited to 15,000 copies
No. **LIBRARY**

Photograph by Theodore Wilson

The former Chickasaw National Capitol Building, which has served in recent years as the Johnston County courthouse in Tishomingo, Oklahoma.

THE

CHICKASAW

PEOPLE

by W. David Baird

Scientific Editor: Henry F. Dobyns
General Editor: John I. Griffin

PUBLISHED BY INDIAN TRIBAL SERIES / PHOENIX

ABOUT THE CHICKASAW GOVERNOR

OVERTON JAMES (Indian name - Itoahtubbi) was born July 21, 1925, in Bromide, Oklahoma. The son of Rufus (Cub) James and Vinnie May Sealey James, both enrolled Chickasaws, he was reared in Wapanucka, Oklahoma, where he graduated from high school in 1942. After two and one-half years in the United States Navy, James returned to Oklahoma and resumed his education at Southeastern State College in Durant. Graduating with a B. A. degree in education in 1949, he taught and coached for ten years in schools at Ravia, Caddo, and Shattuck. In 1955 he earned a Master's degree from Southeastern. Today he is Director of Indian Education for the State of Oklahoma.

In 1963 Overton James was appointed the 27th Governor of the Chickasaw Nation, the youngest ever to hold that position. He has combined unselfish service to his own tribe with service to all American Indians. He is past president (for four terms) of the Inter-Tribal Council of the Five Civilized Tribes, president of the Choctaw-Chickasaw Confederation, past chairman of the State Indian Affairs Commission, trustee of the National Indian Athletic Hall of Fame, member of the Indian Education Subcommittee of the National Council on

Indian Opportunity, and member of the National Congress of American Indians.

Governor James and his wife, Evelyn, maintain a residence in Oklahoma City. They are the parents of one daughter, Ranell, now Mrs. Bill Rostochil.

Photograph by Curtis

THE TWENTY-SEVENTH GOVERNOR of the Chickasaw Nation, Overton James.

ONE APRIL MORNING in 1952 two men waited for an elevator in the southeast basement corner of the Oklahoma state capitol building. One was Johnston Murray, governor of the state, and the other was Earl Welch, justice of the state Supreme Court. In addition to being public servants, these two men had something else in common; they were Chickasaw Indians. On similar mornings twenty-one years later, Overton James, the State Director of Indian Education, waits for the same elevator. He too is a Chickasaw; indeed, he is the Governor of the Chickasaw Nation. Though many know of the accomplishments of these gentlemen, few recognize the significance of their Indian heritage. As Chickasaws, they are heirs of a proud tradition, they are descendants of a special people who have always merited the recognition of their

U.S. BUREAU OF INDIAN AFFAIRS MUSKOGEE AREA Director Virgil N. Harrington (r. wearing glasses) administers the oath of office as Governor of the Chickasaw Nation to Overton James (l.). First popularly elected Governor of the Chickasaw Nation since Oklahoma statehood, James is also the youngest of its twenty-seven Governors

on taking office. In this October, 1971, ceremony, Mrs. James stands on the Governor's left, and his mother, Mrs. Vinnie Humes, holds the Bible upon which his left hand rests.

peers. In positions of prominence, therefore, the governor, the judge, and the educator only follow the paths of their fathers. That the past can shape the present is a truth little acknowledged by the "now" generation. At a time when America has lost sight of her national purpose, she would do well to recall the Chickasaw story, a saga of loyalty, pride, discipline, and preservation.

THE CHILDREN OF ABABINILI

The Chickasaws are a people of great antiquity. Tribal legends record a genesis somewhere in the distant west in the land of the Setting Sun. For some unexplained reason at the dawn of history they left the home of their nativity and began a long and difficult quest for another homeland. Their guide on this journey was a sacred pole which each evening was placed upright in the ground. At morning's light the pole was found leaning toward the east, in which direction the tribe faithfully marched. Eventually the ancient Chickasaws crossed the Mississippi River and came to the banks of the Tennessee River. At that location the pole remained upright, a phenomenon the tribe's holy men took as a signal to terminate their wanderings and to establish new homes. With great rejoicing they built settlements and planted corn in what became Chickasaw Old Fields. In due time, however, the pole stirred

4

again, pointing westward, and once more the tribe resumed its trek. In the Tombigbee highlands near present Tupelo, Mississippi, the pole again stood erect, whereupon the Chickasaw Old Fields were restored. From that point the tribe dispersed to control an area bounded on the north by the Ohio, on the east by the Tennessee, on the south by Okitibbeha Creek, a tributary of the Tombigbee, and on the west by the Mississippi River.

Early European accounts of the Chickasaws give some insight as to the nature of life in their Mississippi homeland. Like their aboriginal neighbors to the southeast, they spoke a language since classified as Muskogean. Described as tall and well built with reddish brown skin, coal black hair and large, dark eyes, they were a most attractive people. The warriors shaved the sides of their head, leaving hair sufficient only for a top roach that was dressed in bear grease. They painted their bodies on ceremonial occasions, and they frequently ornamented themselves with ear and nose rings and eagle and turkey feathers. Chickasaw men were clad in deerskin breechcloths, shirts, and leggings, as well as bearhide moccasins. In the winter they not only wore bison robes but clothes made from the skins of panthers, bears, beavers, and otters. Noted for their "beautiful and clean" appearance and once described as "nymphs of the woods," the women tied up their long hair, which they also dressed in bear's fat. They wore dresses of deerskin gathered at the waist by a leather belt, and in winter wrapped their bodies in softened skins of buffalo calves.

To sustain themselves the early Chickasaws depended primarily upon the bounty of nature. In the forests of their homeland, they hunted deer, bear, and at one time bison. The deer was the most prized for it provided not only meat but material for clothing, arrow points, bow strings, and thread. Hunters esteemed the bear as well, which supplied warm robes and abundant oil for cooking and body rubs. From the verdant forests the Chickasaws also gathered plums, persimmons, grapes, mulberries, strawberries, walnuts, chesnuts, acorns, and onions. These natural foods were supplemented with the harvest of cultivated fields. Corn was the principal crop, although kidney beans, pumpkins, squash, and sunflowers were also grown. Together with that taken from the forest, food derived from agriculture provided the Chickasaws with a varied and sumptuous table.

The natural environment also supplied the tribe with material for comfortable housing. Indeed, each family built a winter house, a summer house, a building for the storage of corn, and a menstrual hut. The winter house was a circular structure covered with a mud plaster and containing an earthen floor. The summer house was rectangular, had walls of woven mats, and had a gabled roof covered with bark or grass thatch. The Chickasaws furnished their homes with beds constructed around the walls on elevated frames, with small seats, with wooden dishes, ladles, and spoons, and with large clay pots suitable for storage of food.

The homes of the individual Chickasaws were grouped together to form villages. At least seven in number, some of these towns contained as many as two hundred households. Each had a log palisade fort, grounds for councils, ceremonies, and ball games, and public building for religious and governmental functions. The villages were usually located on one of the intermittent prairies of the Tombigbee highlands. From these communities the Chickasaws, a restless and expansive people, ranged as far east as the Atlantic, as far north as the Great Lakes, as far west as the Great Plains, and as far south as the Gulf of Mexico.

In their forested homeland, the ancient Chickasaws developed a sophisticated social and governmental structure. The tribe was organized into two grand divisions, the *Imosaktcan* and the *Intcukwalipa*. These grand divisions were then sub-divided into seven to fifteen smaller units, known as clans, each of which had descriptive names such as Raccoon, Panther, Alligator, Spanish and Chief *(Minko)*. These various clans were ranked in importance and had ceremonial as well as actual prerogatives, especially on the

7

occasion of a national council. Also, the ranking clan of the *Imosaktcan* division, the *Minko*, selected the High Minko, an official known to Europeans as the King of the Chickasaws. The *Tishu Minko* assisted the principal chief as a trusted adviser and spokesman in the national council. The latter body was composed of chiefs selected by each clan and of distinguished elder Chickasaws and met at the call of the High Minko at Chukafalaya, the site of the national council house. Though a prestigeous group, the council provided the tribal king more with advice than with legislative enactments.

These governmental patterns were of utmost importance, but the family unit provided the real foundation of Chickasaw society. Men selected their wives from the same grand division but from different clans. Marriage occurred when the bridegroom took a choice ear of corn and before two witnesses divided it with his bride, or lacking the corn presented a deer's foot to his intended. After the bride served the groom some cakes of bread, the two went "to bed like an honest couple." Child betrothals, temporary unions, divorce and polygamy were practiced by the Chickasaws. Neither was adultry uncommon, for which the woman could be whipped, her hair shorn and her face disfigured. The man usually escaped punishment for such an involvement. The children of the marriage union were reckoned to be of the mother's

8

division and clan, making Chickasaw society matrilineal. Growing up in relative freedom they were disciplined only infrequently. On those rare occasions the mother looked to the girls, while the oldest uncle of the mother's clan corrected the boys.

The early Chickasaws manifested a deep religious faith. They directed their devotion to a supreme being, *Ababinili,* who was the author of all life and who "guided them and told them what to do." Dwelling in the heavens, *Ababinili* nontheless manifested himself on earth in the form of a sacred fire watched by guardian priests. The tribe also recognized numerous lesser deities. There were evil giants *(lonfas)* and helpful pygmies *(iyaganasha),* and there was reverence for rattlesnakes and fear of owls. When individual Chickasaws died, they ascended to the heavens if they had lived an exemplary life; to the void of the distant west if they had been evil. The mysteries of *Ababinili* and life after death were plumbed by two Beloved Holy Men, the *Hopaye,* one chosen from each of the two grand divisions of the tribe. Assisted by lesser priests, they sought to be the instruments and the interpreters of the life forces operative in the universe. They presided at tribal ceremonies, supervised religious observances, and advised leaders on questions of national importance.

Among those ceremonies supervised by the

Beloved Holy Men, two stand out as most important. The busk festival was observed annually in the summer months when the green corn was ripe and was for the purpose of national renewal and perpetuation of health. The Chickasaws remembered *Ababinili*, fasted, purged and purified their bodies, feasted on roasting ears, and enjoyed dances, games, and general merrymaking. Tribal leaders also used the occasion to conduct national business. Distinguished warriors were recognized, pardons were granted to criminals, and youths were instructed in tradition and lore. An occasion of similar importance was the Picofa ceremony. Its purpose, though, was to restore a sick person to health.

Social events with somewhat less religious and curative significance also characterized the lifeways of the early Chickasaws. These were usually dominated by games such as *toli* and *chunkey*, played only by men, and *akabatle*, engaged in by both men and women. Resembling lacrosse, the game of toli was played on a court about 500 feet long with a goal at each end. Toli players used two rackets and a ball of stuffed deerskin; the object of the game was for one team to throw the ball through their opponents' goal. Chunkey was played by throwing lances at a rolling stone. The one who threw his lance closest to the stone when it came to a rest won. In akabatle men and women gathered about a single pole and attempted to

10

TE ATA (MARY THOMPSON), noted Chickasaw dancer during the 1920's.

strike an object atop the pole with a ball. Feasts and merriment followed the conclusion of the different games.

Of all the social characteristics of the early Chickasaws, the most notable was their martial spirit. As the English trader James Adair wrote: "they are the readiest, and the quickest of all people in going to shed blood." On these occasions small groups of warriors usually of a single clan sought the favor of *Ababinili* through a three-day fast, during which they regularly purged their bodies with a specially brewed potion. In the course of the fast they prepared medicine bundles and inspected their implements of war. At its conclusion they were addressed by a venerable old warrior who exhorted them to be courageous, watchful, fleet of foot, unfailing in endurance, cunning as a fox, sleepless as a wolf, and agile as a panther. A special dance terminated preparations for the expedition. Upon its return to its village, a successful war party was met with great ceremony and general rejoicing. Such enthusiasm instilled a pride that made the Chickasaws an unconquerable people, totally unwilling to be subservient to an alien power.

THE BELOVED WARRIORS, 1540 – 1783

The Chickasaws remained uncorrupted in their natural ways until 1540. On December 14 of that year, however, there appeared on the south bank of the Tombigbee River a column of men mounted on awesome four legged animals and protected by gleaming armor. This, of course, was the command of Herando de Soto, a Spanish expedition which the previous year had landed at Tampa Bay and had thereafter wandered across much of what is now the southeastern United States. These sons of Spain were wholly unwelcomed among the 5,000 Chickasaws, yet their leader demanded that the tribe provide accommodations, food and women. Throughout the winter the unwilling hosts of the Europeans complied with the increasingly repugnant requests, but by March 4, 1541, they had had enough. Early that morning the Chickasaws fell upon de Soto's party, set fire to its dwellings, killed twelve of its members, and destroyed fifty to sixty of its horses. The rout would have been complete had not the attackers mistaken stampeding horses for a mustering of cavalry. Though they repulsed a later second attack, the Spaniards hastened their preparations to continue their westward journey. By April 26, the intruders had gone to meet an uncertain fate beyond the Mississippi River. In their wake the Chickasaws had reason to congratulate themselves and to issue thanksgiving to *Ababinili*.

The four month confrontation with the Spanish expedition was of importance in that it

13

signaled the beginning of an international contest for the control of the lower Mississippi Valley. In due time other European powers arrived in the New World to challenge the pretensions of Spain. Settling Charles Town in 1670, British citizens engaged in a vigorous trade with the Indians and within a decade had reached the Chickasaws on the Tennessee River. Traders such as Thomas Welch and Anthony Dodsworth brought guns and ammunition, cutting tools, creature comforts, and clothing. For these coveted items, the tribe could barter only two natural resources — deerskins and slaves.

The Chickasaw-English trade had significant implications for both parties. On the one hand, the demand for deerskins changed the hunting practices of the Indians. Where they had hunted only for food and clothing, they now stalked the deer for profit and power. Where once the region adjacent to their villages had supplied their economic needs, they now pushed beyond that area to intrude on the hunting ranges of their neighbors. Similarly, the demand of the British colonists for slaves intensified the warlike character of the tribe, for only in war could the captives be secured for sale into bondage. For that reason the Chickasaws sent slave hunting parties southward to the Choctaws, expeditions that in 1690 stimulated a war of some twelve years in duration and produced more than 500 salable captives. On the other hand, the trade proved immensely profitable to the Carolinians. In 1707, southern Indians produced some 121,000 skins for shipment to England; in 1748 approximately 160,000 were exported.

Though the slave trade was less profitable economically, it was just as significant strategically. So successful was the commerce in skins that English officials early envisioned an expansion of their empire to the Mississippi Valley. If those plans were to succeed, the Indian Nations allied with any competing power would have to be eliminated. The Chickasaw slave traffic, therefore, was beneficial largely because it broke down barriers to Anglo advance.

The principal competitor of Britain in the West was France. Since 1673 when Father Marquette and Louis Joliet drifted down the Father of Waters, the French had claimed the entire Mississippi basin as their special province. Not until 1699, however, were they able to establish a permanent outpost at Biloxi and another three years later at Mobile Bay. Their push to the Gulf of Mexico stemmed in large part from their desire to thwart the westward expansion of Britain from Carolina. Governor Pierre Le Moyne d' Iberville believed, however, that more than mere settlement of the Gulf Coast was required to meet the British threat. The Indians, especially the Chickasaws, must be won to the banner of the French sovereign.

Iberville hoped to win the Indians by a policy of peace and commerce. Calling the Chickasaws and Choctaws to Mobile in 1702, he urged the former to halt their slave raids and to expell resident English traders. He threatened to arm the enemies of the Chickasaws if they refused, but he promised protection, trade, and missionaries if they complied. Always a practical people and not yet irrevocably committed to Britain, the Chickasaws agreed to accept French protection and commerce. Rather than admit any missionaries, however, the tribe permitted Iberville to send St. Michael, a fourteen year old youth, to live with it. The youngster presumably would learn the ways of the tribe, but in reality he was to encourage the Indians to remain faithful to the new alliance.

Far from solidifying France's position in the Mississippi Valley, the Mobile agreement only intensified the competition for empire. Britain was determined to retain her toe-hold in the West, an implacement that in large measure depended upon her ability to effect a lasting accord with the Chickasaws. Horses laden with trade goods set out from Charles Town for the tribal domain. Arms and munitions were distributed among the Chickasaws, and British traders took up permanent residence among them. Soon the war against the French-allied Choctaws was resumed, only this time as a part

16

of a broader colonial conflict between France and England known as Queen Anne's War. In the fall of 1705 a combined Chickasaw-Creek force of 300 warriors led by British nationals marched through the Choctaw country, laid waste their villages and fields and took numerous captives that were later sold as slaves. Again in 1711, Thomas Welch headed a Chickasaw party of 200 braves that rained destruction upon the populous Choctaw towns.

Any advantage the British colonials won by promoting such raids was negated by the brilliant diplomacy of Jean Baptiste le Moyne d' Bienville, the brother and successor of Governor Iberville. Gracious in manner and fluent in aboriginal language, Bienville in 1712 negotiated a settlement between the Chickasaws and Choctaws. The peace that followed enabled the French to regain their influence among the Choctaws, which, at the conclusion of Queen Anne's War in 1713, insured their continued survival in the Mississippi Valley. It did not, however, induce the Chickasaws to expell the British. For the sons of France, therefore, the peace could be no more than a prelude to continued conflict.

In the decade that followed, the British influence among the Chickasaws so increased that raids on French settlements and allied Indians became the rule rather than the exception. Convinced that France would know no

17

peace until the British menance was eliminated, Bienville, in January, 1723, purchased the services of Choctaw mercenaries and initiated an all-out offensive against the Chickasaws. According to the French, the attackers dealt the British allies a grievous blow, returning to their villages with 400 scalps and 100 prisoners. Even if the statistics were inflated, the Chickasaws were terribly hurt by the attack. One band left to live with the Cherokees, another departed for the Creeks, and still another led by Squirrel King sought safety on the Savannah River. The remainder, though, took revenge upon the French and harrassed commerce on the Mississippi between Illinois and New Orleans. Simultaneously, the Chickasaws sent emmissaries to the Choctaws asking why they were lackeys of the French and promising trade with the British if hostilities ceased. Weary of the war, the Choctaws appealed to their benefactors to negotiate a settlement. Concerned about the interdiction of commerce and convinced that the honor of France had been sustained, Bienville acceded to the request and arranged the desired accommodation.

If the Governor had hoped to profit from his diplomacy, he was sadly mistaken. Aware that the Chickasaws held the key to their ambitions in the West, British officials determined to expand greatly their trade in and through the nation. They planned to make their villages entrepots for trade goods to be introduced to tribes allied with the French. To be sure the additional commerce would bring increased prosperity, but more importantly it would decrease the dependence of the Indians upon Mobile. The British plan worked beyond all expectations. Operating surreptitiously, the Chickasaw traders so influenced the Natchez Indians that on November 28, 1729, warriors of that tribe fell upon the French garrisons at Fort Rosalie and Fort St. Peter on the Mississippi River. At least 250 Frenchmen were killed and 300 women and children were taken captive. A combined Choctaw-French force avenged the raid the following year and recovered most of the hostages. Though most of the Natchez were slain, some 200 survivors took refuge among the Chickasaws.

The disaster at Fort Rosalie stirred the French to retaliatory measures other than just punishing the perpetrators of the plot. Aware of the role of the Chickasaws, Mobile officials obtained the assistance of Illinois Indians who in 1732 and 1733 carried out a series of attacks upon the Chickasaw villages. These raids, though, only provoked the Chickasaws to prey upon French river commerce and to initiate a campaign to bring the Choctaws within the English orbit. Given this response, Bienville determined that France's policy had not been sufficiently punitive. "The entire destruction of [the Chick-

19

asaws]," he concluded, "becomes every day more necessary to our interests and I am going to exert all diligence to accomplish it."

True to his word, Bienville made plans to muster all available French military resources and personally lead a campaign against the offending Indians. In preparation for the attack he stockpiled supplies, sent spies into the Chickasaw country, and ordered construction of Fort Tombeckbe in the Choctaw Nation to provide cover for the advance. He also directed Major Pierre D' Artaguette to gather local French forces in the Illinois region and to rendezvous with his army in the enemy's domain. On April 4, 1736, Bienville left Mobile with a 600 man expedition that included French and Swiss regulars, local militia, volunteers and forty-five Negroes. Sixteen days later at Fort Tombeckbe he was met by 600 Choctaw mercenaries.

Even before Bienville left Mobile, Major D 'Artaguette had landed his 400 man army at Chickasaw Bluffs on the Mississippi. For twenty-one days in February, 1736, he attempted to make a connection with the French forces presumably marching north from the Gulf. Failing, he was persuaded to make an attack upon the Chickasaw town of Chocolissa. He would have been better advised to return to Illinois without doing battle. The Chickasaws cut his army to ribbons. Only twenty escaped.

20

The remainder, including D'Artaguette and Father Antoine Senat, were burned alive.

Unaware of this disaster, Bienville crossed the Tombigbee River and in late May, 1736, arrived before the town of Akia near modern Tupelo. After studying the Indian defenses, he ordered an attack on the twenty-sixth. At three o'clock in the afternoon the French marched toward the Chickasaw defenders in classic European formation. Though they carried a forward palisade, a deadly crossfire checked any further advance of the attackers. After three hours of battle, Bienville called for a retreat, and he and his forces returned to the safety of the Choctaw Nation. How the Chickasaws reacted to their victory was not recorded. Yet surely they took pride in their defeat of so formidable a foe and again gave thanks to their maker and protector, *Ababinili.*

Bienville, though, was not finished. He intensified his efforts to bring the Chickasaws to terms and to expel their British allies. He no more than returned to Mobile than he planned a second invasion. This time, however, he expected to muster 1200 regular and militia troops and 1500 northern and southern Indian auxiliaries. A forward post was established at Chickasaw Bluffs, to which Bienville repaired in September, 1739, with four eight-pound cannon, eight four-pound cannon, 2000 grenades, 50,000 pounds of powder, 60,000 pounds of bullets,

200 horses and a 3600 man army. Altogether it was the largest military force ever drawn before an Indian adversary in the West. Even at that, the French met with little success. One column was forced to lift a two-day siege of a Chickasaw town. The rest of the army bogged down in the rain-soaked terrain. To save the honor of the expedition, the governor in desperation invited the Chickasaws to treat with him. In February, 1740, a tribal delegation began negotiations which resulted in a decision to end hostilities and exchange prisoners. After this anti-climax, Bienville ordered the removal of his army from the Chickasaw domain. Thus, for the second time in four years the tribe had repulsed a French force bent on destruction. In preserving itself, of course, it had also preserved the British interest in the Mississippi Valley. No wonder James Adair, a Carolina trader, saw the Chickasaws as "Beloved Warriors."

Bienville's failure before Akia and the Chickasaw Bluffs brought his dismissal and replacement by the Marquis de Vaudreuil. The new governor assumed his duties on the eve of King George's War which provided the pretext to continue attempts to annihilate the Chickasaws and to expell the British. To this end he sought to bestir the Choctaws to attack their northern neighbor, but British traders so effectively worked among these French allies that they not only nullified the request but induced a debilitating civil war. Vaudreuil did succeed in instigating an attack by a band of Pennsylvania Shawnees, but the Chickasaws repulsed it with little loss. Although King George's War ended in 1748, presumably terminating the conflict between Great Britain and France, the governor was so frustrated in his efforts to exterminate the "Beloved Warriors" that he extended his efforts into the next decade. In 1752 he invaded the tribal domain with 700 regulars and a large number of Indian auxiliaries. As the Chickasaws remained behind their defenses, Vaudreuil could only burn fields and drive off livestock.

The one-half century contest between the French and the British-allied Chickasaws was, of course, only a small part of a larger effort to win control of the whole of the North American continent. Events well east of the Mississippi River determined the conclusion of the broader conflict. In the so-called French and Indian War, the more numerous British population on the Atlantic Coast and the superiority of King George's navy spelled the defeat of French arms. Far removed from the military activity, the Chickasaws could only applaud the success of their patrons and rejoice with them in the terms of the Peace of Paris in 1763. By its provisions France withdrew from North America, ceding her possessions east of the Mississippi to England and those west of the river to Spain. For the

Chickasaws, their commitment to a British alliance some sixty years previously had proved the better part of wisdom.

In order to solidify their control of their new acquisition, English officials called the southeastern tribes to a conference at Augusta in November, 1763, and at Mobile in March, 1765. At both conclaves Superintendent of Southern Indians John Stuart greeted the Chickasaws led by Piomingo as worthy allies and commended their loyalty as an example to other tribes. Stuart praised them as "generous friends. . .whom neither dangers could startle nor promises seduce from our interests." Furthermore, the Indian policy announced and later implemented by Stewart proved beneficial in the short run to the tribe. The proclamation line drawn in 1763 placed the Chickasaw domain well beyond the region approved for legitimate white settlement. The quality of trade goods improved and rules regulating commerce were established. Stuart even assigned John McIntosh as his personal deputy to live within the Chickasaw Nation and to minister to the tribe's needs. More importantly, in the absence of French intrigue British policy engendered an era of relative peace and quiet. A major exception occurred in 1765 when Chickasaw warriors participated in a British led attack on Illinois Indians during the course of Pontiac's famous rebellion.

That the Chickasaws continued to esteem the English nation proved most beneficial for the Europeans upon the advent of the American revolution. At first inclined to keep all Indians neutral, British officials early turned to them for military assistance. To thwart any revolutionary activity in the West, in December, 1775, Stuart sent 3,000 pounds of powder and a large supply of lead to the Chickasaw towns. In May, 1777, Piomingo and Mingo Homa led forty warriors to Mobile to reaffirm tribal allegiance to Britain. The delegation received instructions to watch the Mississippi River and to prevent any American effort similar to that of George Rogers Clark on the Ohio. Though the Chickasaws in February, 1778, permitted the James Willing expedition to go unimpeded, when Virginians in 1780 attempted to establish Fort Jefferson on Chickasaw Bluffs tribal warriors led by James Colbert, an intermarried trader, so harrassed the post that it was abandoned the following year.

Chickasaw involvement in the Revolutionary struggle became even more pronounced once the Spanish sovereigns of New Orleans and the west bank of the Mississippi, entered the conflict. After a declaration of war on Great Britain, the Spanish Governor of Louisiana led armies that captured Baton Rouge, Natchez, Mobile, and finally Pensacola. Indeed, by mid-1781, the Chickasaw Nation remained the only stronghold of Britain in the West. As such, it became the haven for English refugees, individuals who joined tribal warriors in raids on American and Spanish positions. So effective were the Beloved Warriors that they virtually closed down commerce on the Mississippi. In May, 1782, for example, a party led by Colbert intercepted a river convoy, capturing the wife and family of the lieutenant governor of Spanish Illinois. The following year, Fort Carlos on the Arkansas River fell to Chickasaw arms.

Spain, however, did not permit such attacks to go unchallenged. She inspired Illinois Indians to raid the villages of the Chickasaws. And in the summer of 1782 a Spanish army landed at Chickasaw Bluffs, wreaking considerable havoc. For that matter, Principal Chief Payamataha so wearied of the retaliation in specific and the war in general that he journeyed to St. Louis to seek some kind of accommodation. Most of his people, however, viewed the Spaniards as anathama and rather than make a peace with them preferred to come to terms with the Americans. Accordingly, Piomingo and James Colbert entered into negotiations with commissioners from Virginia, signing in November, 1783, a treaty that called for peace, expulsion of hostile Europeans, and return of American prisoners. Such an agreement was propitious as military disasters on the Atlantic had forced Britain earlier that same year to recognize American independence and to yield

26

her claims to the area east of the Mississippi River. For the Beloved Warriors the Peace of Paris meant that a century long association with the English King had ended and that an era of uncertainty had dawned.

The feeling of uncertainty stemmed from more than just an altered political climate. The one hundred years of intimate European contact had significantly changed traditional patterns of conduct. Once self-sufficient and independent, the Chickasaws had come to depend upon manufactured implements. Tribal hunters had always found game plentiful in adjacent territory, but commercial demands now necessitated hunts well beyond the ancestral domain. Though the famous Chickasaw horse facilitated these expeditions, their success was never assured. Furthermore, the coming of the Europeans brought the introduction of customs hitherto unknown. Especially significant was the distribution of brandy and rum, brews that debauched many proud warriors. Also, a number of white men took up permanent residence among the Indians, intermarried, and produced large mixed-blood families. These opted for a European style of existence, established plantations, and introduced Negro slaves. In due time, they came to exert more influence within the tribe than their number warranted.

Traditional Chickasaw patterns were also adversely affected by the long international contest for control of the Mississippi Valley. Allied with Britain, tribal thirst for combat was nearly insatiable. Though usually victorious, the Chickasaws lost many of their own people. To maintain their strength the tribe was driven to adopt both captives and remnants of friendly tribes. This mingling of alien blood made it difficult by the end of the eighteenth century to find an "uncorrupted" Chickasaw. In addition to warfare, the international rivalry also severed the ancient unity of the tribal council fire. Though most of the leading men supported Britain, some committed themselves to the ambitions of France or Spain. Civil war was always averted, but the conflict of loyalties left the Chickasaws divided in national purpose.

Though many traditional patterns were seriously altered, some remained unchanged. Foremost was the continued trust placed in *Ababinili.* On more than one occasion the Chickasaws were reminded of the blessings provided by devotion to their maker. Such steadfastness, they no doubt believed, had resulted in their defeat of de Soto, their victories over the French before Akia and the Chickasaw Bluffs, and their fruitful commerce with the British. Accordingly, they had no desire to desert him. Offers to send Christian missionaries were rejected; indeed, one was burned alive. As the Chickasaws assessed it, with their traditions in disarray *Ababinili* alone provided continuity with the past.

THE AMERICANS ARRIVE,
1783 – 1838

The era following American independence saw the continuation of international intrigue among the Chickasaws. Left in control of Louisiana and the Gulf Coast by the Treaty of Paris, Spain was determined to protect her possessions from unfriendly forces, especially restless American frontiersmen. For its part, the United States saw the control of the Mississippi Valley as vital to its economic growth and prosperity. Both governments hoped to woo the Indians to their respective ambitions by promises of protection and commerce.

As their own well-being depended upon a vigorous trade, the Chickasaws proved susceptible to such overtures. As it had in the past, though, the tribe divided over which power could best provide the goods required. Vigorously anti-American, King Taski Etoka (Hare-lip) and war chief Uguh Yaccbe (Wolf's friend) concluded that only the Spanish licensed firm of Panton, Leslie, and Company could meet the nation's commercial requirements. On the other hand, Piomingo determined that those needs could best be supplied by the Americans.

The division of the tribe into factions that supported either Spain or the United States began as early as 1784. At Mobile in June of that year Spain won from tribal leaders a pledge to keep peace with neighboring Indians and to admit no unauthorized traders. To counter this diplomatic initiative, the Americans two years later called the Chickasaws led by Piomingo to Hopewell, South Carolina, and promised to establish a trading post for the tribe's benefit on the Tennessee River. Spanish officials, as a consequence, redoubled their efforts and prodded Panton, Leslie, and Company to begin immediate operations in the nation. Moreover, Governor Esteban Miro sent Juan de Villebeuvre to live with the Indians as his personal representative. And Miro's successor, Baron de Carondelet, even lent moral support to King Taski Etoka in his plan to form a confederation of southern tribes to check American expansion.

President George Washington viewed this growth of Spanish influence among the Chickasaws with increasing apprehension. Already pressed by the British-inspired Shawnees in the northwest, the United States could hardly afford another Indian conflict on the Mississippi. Accordingly, Washington appointed James Robertson, a Tennessee resident, as tribal agent and in 1792 directed the governor of the southern territory, James Blount, to assemble tribal leaders in Nashville in an effort to check the Spaniards. Blount's assignment was made easier by the fact that Piomingo and fifty of his warriors had the previous year joined the Americans in a

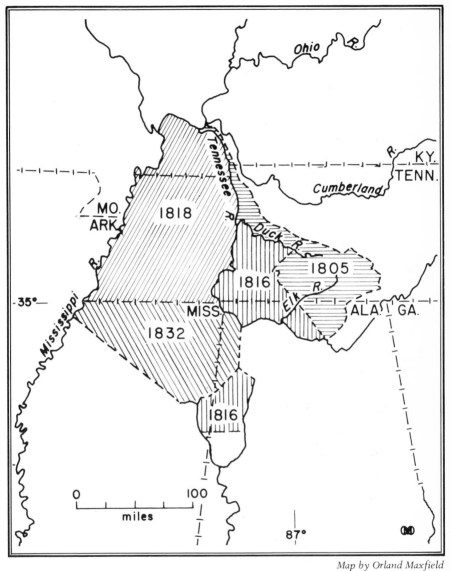

Map by Orland Maxfield

MAP 1. Chickasaw land cessions to the United States of America between 1800 and removal to Indian Territory.

campaign against the Shawnees. He therefore easily parlayed this manifestation of loyalty into a formal declaration of intent to live in peace with the United States.

Two years later American officials received their first dividend from the new alliance. Sixty Chickasaws served valiantly with General Anthony Wayne at Fallen Timbers, an effort wholly unappreciated by the citizens of Cincinnati. They stoned the warriors who passed through their city after the battle. President Washington, though, was more gracious. When Piomingo and other chiefs journeyed to Philadelphia to interview him, he gave a written guarantee of Chickasaw boundaries as described by the chiefs.

These expressions of tribal allegiance to the United States only encouraged Spanish officials to renew their efforts to win the Chickasaws. Supported completely by the anti-American chief, Ugula Yaccbe, they worked to reduce the influence of Piomingo. In May, 1795, Governor Carondelet even built Fort San Fernando at Chickasaw Bluffs and opened a trading house operated by Panton, Leslie, and Company. His efforts, however, were in vain, but not because the Chickasaws failed to respond to Spanish diplomacy. In 1796 Spain signed the Treaty of San Lorenzo, by which she ceded to the United States her claims to territory north of thirty-one degrees and east of the Mississippi River. The terms of the treaty, therefore, obligated Carondelet to abandon Fort San Fernando as well as his quest for the allegiance of the Chickasaws.

The withdrawal of Spain from the tribal domain was something less than a total blessing for the tribe. Her presence had served as a counterpoise to the expansive designs of the United States. Now that Spain had gone, little remained to check the desire of restless Americans for more land. For the Chickasaws, these circumstances prior to 1818 meant four treaties by which their boundaries were either redefined or reduced. An 1801 agreement drew borders for the tribe, while one in 1805 secured a cession of that land north of the Tennessee River. An 1886 treaty extinguished tribal title to lands between the Tennessee and Tombigbee Rivers. Then the demanding Treaty of 1818 deprived the tribe of its remaining domain in eastern Tennessee.

Why did the Chickasaws agree to these cessions? Really, they had little choice, and given the circumstances, they made the best bargain possible. One method used by the government was wholesale bribery, or, as Andrew Jackson put it, "...touching their interest, and feeding their avarice." In the Treaty of 1805, for example, George Colbert and Tishumastubbee were paid $1,000 each, while King Chinubbee Minko was granted $100 a year for life. To secure the accord of 1886, United States commissioners surreptitiously distributed $4,500 to influential Chickasaws, while from $100 to $150 was paid to each chief in 1818. To win these treaties of cession, government representatives also feted, threatened, and withheld annuities previously pledged by the United States.

Though bribery played a role in the Treaty of 1816, there was a more significant impetus — the famous Creek War of 1813-1814. Encouraged by the brilliant Shawnee leader, Tecumseh, conservative Creeks — known as Red Sticks — massacred a white and mixed-blood settlement at Fort Mims, Alabama. Having previously rejected Tecumseh's message, some 350 Chickasaw warriors eagerly joined General Andrew Jackson's white and Indian troops to destroy the Red Sticks at Horseshoe Bend and other battles. In the peace treaty that followed, Jackson used the rebellion as a pretext to extort from the Creeks a major portion of their ancestral domain. Part of the ceded lands, however, clearly belonged to the Chickasaw Nation. When tribal protests fell on deaf ears, the Chickasaws could do no more than endorse the Creek cession and salvage in 1816 as much compensation as possible.

The treaties that reduced the Chickasaw domain to northwestern Mississippi had resulted primarily from settler pressure for more land. By

34

accommodating these demands, the tribe hoped to be done with the non-Indian and his ambitions. Yet after 1818 the number of whites within and adjacent to the Chickasaw Nation continued to increase. This alien presence had a profound impact upon the nature of Chickasaw society and the course of tribal history. Recently arrived whites intermarried and took advantage of the tribal practice of holding the land in common to establish large plantations cultivated by slave labor. Moreover, they sired large mixed-blood families who came to control the political and economic life of the nation. The more important families included the Colberts, the Loves, the Harrises, and the McIntoshes. The ascendency of the mixed bloods meant that the full bloods withdrew either physically or emotionally from the mainstream of tribal life.

The economic life of the nation was also affected by the non-Indian presence. Chickasaws who once stalked the deer and bear found that the hunt yielded only small game and turkeys. Though some of the more enterprising did assume the role of middle men in a lucrative trade with western Indians, most turned to agriculture. Abandoning their traditional villages, they spread out over the intermittent prairies where the full bloods established subsistence-type farms and the mixed bloods created prosperous cotton plantations. Some mixed bloods also operated ferries, grinding mills, and blacksmith and mechanic shops.

As in social and economic affairs, the non-Indian influence also reshaped traditional governmental patterns of the Chickasaws. Though the hereditary king and council of clan chiefs was retained, the real political power was exercised by the mixed bloods. So politically astute were they that in 1829 the council adopted a code of written laws which, among other things, gave special protection to private property.

The increasingly tenuous ties with the past were further weakened after 1820 when Christian missionaries arrived to do battle with *Ababinili*. Alexander Deavers and Alexander Talley carried the cross for the Methodists, while John Ficklin, Stark Dupuy, and J. A. Ware labored for the Baptists. The Presbyterians, however, made the most concerted effort among the Chickasaws, and typically they were as much interested in education as in evangelism. Due to their efforts, two schools — Clarity Hall and Monroe — were opened, and through their influence the tribal council subsidized three other institutions — Tokshis, Martyn, and Caney Creek. On the whole, though, this early mission effort was largely unsuccessful: probably three of every four converts were Negro slaves and all of the schools had closed by 1834. Still, the missionaries did try to protect the Indians from settler exploitation and many Chickasaws received a rudimentary education in their schools.

Probably the most significant aspect of the non-Indian presence was the resultant demand for additional cessions of land. Lusting after the tribe's fertile acres, settlers on the rim of the Chickasaw Nation pressured the federal government to remove the Indians from the remainder of their ancestral domain. American officials were not unresponsive. Indeed, since the acquisition of Louisiana in 1803, they had envisioned the removal of all eastern Indians beyond the Mississippi. Not until 1826, however, did the Chickasaws consent to discuss such proposals, and then only to reject them. Hoping to entice the tribe to emigrate, Commissioner of Indian Affairs Thomas McKenney the following year persuaded the tribe to send an exploring party to visit the western lands. Traversing Indian Territory in 1828, this group was not impressed with the terrain, reinforcing the tribe's determination not to abandon their ancient homeland and prosperous farms.

Two important events, however, broke the Chickasaw resolve to remain in Mississippi. In 1830, President Andrew Jackson pushed through Congress the Indian Removal Act which provided for the compulsory removal of eastern tribes to the West. More importantly, during the same period the states of Mississippi and Alabama acted to abolish tribal governments, authorized fines for those leaders who resisted, and declared all Indians subject to state laws. Clearly unconstitutional, these measures were nonetheless endorsed by federal officials. So, the Chickasaws, if they were to continue as a separate people, had to submit to removal.

The diplomacy precedent to physical removal began at Franklin, Tennessee, in August, 1830. There the Chicksaws agreed to cede their homeland for one in the West. Each person was to receive a specified land allotment in fee simple, which would be sold if he emigrated and taxable if he remained. The United States agreed to pay an annuity, the expenses of removal, and subsistence for one year. The treaty, though, would be operative only if the Chickasaws found a suitable home in the West. The latter proviso proved the undoing of the Franklin accord, as an exploring party headed by Levi Colbert reported in May, 1831, that it had found no land satisfactory to the needs of the Chickasaws.

Liberated from its initial agreement, the tribe entered into new negotiations with the United States in October, 1832. The resultant treaty signed at the tribal council house on Pontotoc Creek committed the Chickasaws to the cession of the tribal domain. The land would be surveyed and sold by the government and the net proceeds of the sale paid to the nation. Until

38

a new country was found west of the river, every family could select from one to five sections of the land for its temporary use. Because the tribal treasury would receive the proceeds of all sales, the Chickasaws were to pay for their removal to and subsistence in the West.

The Pontotoc Treaty was no more than signed until it became the subject of considerable controversy. In 1833 and again the following year, Chickasaw delegations traveled to Washington in an effort to secure modifications of the instrument. Finally, in May, 1834, they negotiated an amendment which increased the size of the temporary homesteads and, significantly, granted holders of such allotments a fee simple title, enabling them to dispose of the land and to control the proceeds. The amendment also established a Chickasaw commission to supervise the funds of the nation and those revenues derived from homestead sales by incompetents.

Though they were now committed to removal, the Chickasaws were thwarted in their attempts to emigrate because of their inability to find a new home in the West. Delegations in 1833 and 1835 proposed to the Choctaws that they sell a portion of their western domain to the tribe. The Choctaws rejected these proposals until January, 1837, when they agreed to admit the Chickasaws into their nation with all the rights and privileges of citizenship. Furthermore, they set aside a Chickasaw District in the western portion of their domain, the title to which they insisted be held in common by both tribes. For these rights and privileges, the Chickasaws agreed to pay the Choctaws $530,000 out of their national funds.

With a western homeland now assured, tribal leaders informed the United States they were prepared to emigrate. Indeed, there was some haste to remove. While the Chickasaws had been looking for a home, the federal government had gone ahead with the survey and sale of the 6,422,400 acre Mississippi domain. Consequently, the number of whites in search of land and easy fortune increased significantly. Disputes between the intruders and the Indians were frequent, and transactions between them more often than not left the Red Man debauched, dispossessed, and demoralized. Many Chickasaws, therefore, welcomed the appointment of A. M. M. Upshaw, a Tennesseean, to superintend the tribe's removal to the West.

In preparing for the emigration, Upshaw worked tirelessly. His staff prepared a roll of the tribe, enumerating 4,914 Chickasaws and 1,156 slaves. He contracted for 1,300,000 rations and had them delivered to Memphis, Little Rock, and Fort Coffee, a post on the Arkansas River, just west of Fort Smith. Finally, he announced June 1, 1837, as the date the first emigrant party would head west. Expecting 1,000,

Upshaw was sorely disappointed when only 450 Chickasaws presented themselves on the appointed date. This first party crossed the Mississippi at Memphis on July 4, and traveling on foot reached Little Rock twenty days later. From that point, the conductor, John Millard, expected to follow the Arkansas River to Fort Coffee. Yet three hundred of the emigrants ignored his plans and insisted upon following a southwesterly course from Little Rock to Fort Towson on Red River. When the "recalcitrants" refused to reconsider, Millard left to take those remaining in his charge on to Fort Coffee. He hurried back to Little Rock, however, and found that the larger group had met with continuous troubles. As no rations were available, many had suffered and some had died. In their distress they demonstrated little interest in moving on to Red River. Only by threatening use of the military was Millard able to get the party to hasten its march. It finally reached Fort Towson in early September.

In the second removal Upshaw was determined to overcome the pitfalls of the first. During the summer and fall of 1837 he collected 4,000 Chickasaws in four emigrant camps. In November he started them to Memphis, where he had arranged for boats to transport them down the Mississippi and up the Arkansas to Fort Coffee. All went well until a rumor of a riverboat tragedy that had taken the lives of several hundred other Indians so frightened the emigrants that 1,000 refused to board the waiting boats. Accompanied by some 5,000 horses as well as numerous wagons and teams, these struggled overland across Arkansas reaching Fort Coffee in four to six weeks. The Indians moving by boat reached their destination in only eight to ten days. By early 1838, most of the Chickasaws had arrived in the West, though small parties continued to emigrate for a decade. For example, it was not until mid-1838 that King Ishtehotope joined his people in Indian Territory.

⌐Despite some painful personal losses, the Chickasaw removal was tranquil and orderly, especially when compared to that of the Cherokees. Even at that, it was marred by two massive scandals. Because the tribe paid for its own removal, the government was criminally derelict in its financial and budgetary controls. Subsistence contractors charged excessively for poor quality rations. One investigator found that of the $1.5 million removal cost the Chickasaws were charged $200,000 for spoiled food items and $700,000 for rations never delivered. The scandal over subsistence contracts was of such magnitude that it became the subject of a congressional investigation. The transportation contract was also strongly criticized. The steamboat owner who had contracted to transport members of the second emigration party had

42

received $37,749 in payment for the passage of the 1,000 Chickasaws who refused to travel on his vessel.

LIFE IN THE WEST,
1838 — 1866

Though the scandals attendant to removal distressed the Chickasaws, they were not as important as the life and death challenges confronting the tribe following emigration. Wrenched from familiar surroundings and re-located in a distant land, the Indians were dazed and in some cases helpless. They had no effective leadership as traditional governmental patterns had been suspended during removal. Moreover, emigrants had been capriciously settled with little regard for clan or family in five temporary camps, four of which were located in the Choctaw Nation well east of the Chickasaw District. In these tent cities they suffered from fevers, dysentery, malnutrition, and even smallpox. Debilitated and disorganized, the emigrants demonstrated little interest in abandoning their temporary quarters and re-locating on their assigned reservation. Indeed, in 1844, of the 6,000 Chickasaws who had re-moved more than 4,000 resided in the Choctaw domain.

Several factors accounted for the lack of interest in settling further west. For one thing, the Chickasaws were enervated by their afflu-

43

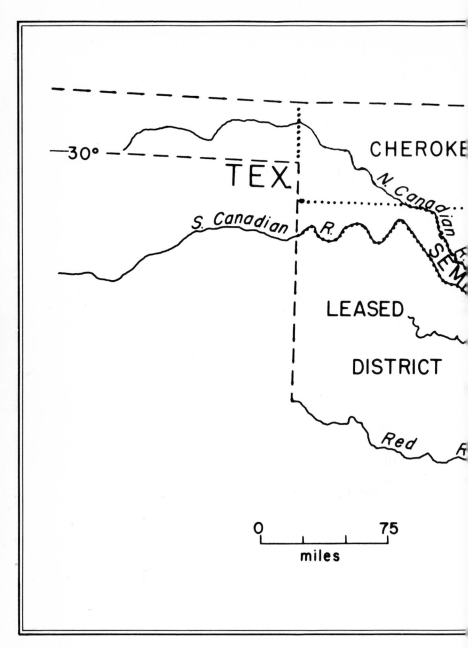

MAP 2. The territory of the Chickasaw Nation and that of the other Civilized Tribes

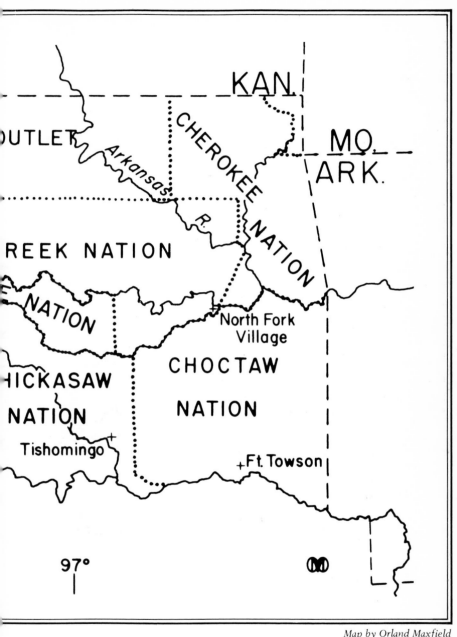

in Indian Territory after removal from the Southeastern states.

ence. Revenue from surplus land sales in Mississippi mounted to over $3,000,000. And even after payment of liberal emigration expenses, the remaining sum yielded an annual interest payment of $60,000 to $75,000. Paid per capita, this money enabled a family of five to receive $75 to $100 per year, which, according to one observer, "induced a general neglect of industry." Finally, Chickasaw ambition to occupy the assigned district was further retarded by the presence there of hostile Plains Indians who threatened the lives and property of those who ventured into the region.

Not unmindful of the plight of the tribe, the federal government acted to enable it to take possession of its new homeland. In 1841, the secretary of war directed Colonel Zachary Taylor to construct Fort Washita just southeast of modern Tishomingo, Oklahoma. Ten years later Captain Randolph B. Marcy established Fort Arbuckle northwest of the older post near present Byars. These two posts significantly reduced the threat of attacks by the frontier tribes, thereby encouraging the Chickasaws to drift into the district assigned to them. By 1858, no more than 1,000 still resided in the Choctaw Nation.

Once settled in their new domain the Chickasaws turned their attention to reconstructing the society so utterly dismembered during removal. In time they developed a satisfactory if

46

not flourishing economy. Holding the land in common, each selected a site for a farm or plantation along one of the many streams that emptied into the Red River. The full bloods usually engaged in subsistence agriculture, planting corn, peas, beans, Irish potatoes, pumpkins, squash, and melons. Some mixed-blood Chickasaws, however, operated large plantations cultivated by slave labor. George Colbert, for example, planted 300 to 500 acres of cotton and employed 150 slaves. So proficient were agricultural operations that the tribe frequently produced a surplus – 40,000 bushels of corn in 1843 alone. Though some of this harvest was sold at military forts, to emigrants traveling to Texas, and in Arkansas, most unfortunately wasted for lack of an adequate market. Tribal agriculture also included stock raising. The Indians used the luxuriant prairie grasses to graze the renowned Chickasaw horse and to fatten large herds of cattle, sheep and goats.

A revitalized commerce was another important aspect of the new economy. Per capita payments and profits from the farm purchased goods imported by white merchant firms such as Saffarans and Lewis and Berthelet, Heald & Company. These concerns focused their activity in communities that grew up in stragetic locations. Those settlements of most importance included Pontotoc, Hatsboro, Colbert, Fort Arbuckle, Tishomingo, and Burney. In addition to commerce, these villages were the centers of significant industrial activity. Enterprising Chickasaws and intermarried white citizens operated grist and saw mills, cotton gins, and ferries. Of the latter, that owned by Benjamin Franklin Colbert on Red River was the most prosperous, providing the proprietor an annual income of $1,000.

As the tribe rebuilt economically, it also sought to pick up the threads of its social life. Two room log houses connected by a dog trot were erected to provide shelters for full bloods. Mixed-blood citizens constructed commodious, plantation-style homes that were the envy of many travelers. After 1854, literate Chickasaws read the *Chickasaw Intelligencer* and its successor, the *Chickasaw and Choctaw Herald,* both of which provided a measure of community cohesion. Though most of the old rituals and dances were lost in the confusion of removal, ball games gave the Chickasaws the opportunity to renew friendships and to discuss issues of national importance. Annuity payments and political gatherings provided similar occasions.

Christian instruction terminated well before emigration, and unlike their behavior toward the Choctaws, the missionaries did not accompany the Chickasaws to the West. Perhaps it was because *Ababinili* retained so many adherents that the preachers deserted them, but whatever the reason they had returned by 1840 to continue their battle with the tribal gods. The Baptists began work among the Chickasaws in 1844, but it was not until 1858 that R. J. Hogue established the Good Springs church, the first congregation of that denomination. Presbyterian missionaries assigned to the Choctaws established a church at Boggy Depot in 1840; three years later they counted 125 communicants among the Chickasaws. Roman Catholic priests attached to the United States Army ministered to the tribe during the 1850's, but the most enduring work was accomplished by the Methodists. E. B. Duncan began his ministry in 1844, establishing a mission at Pleasant Grove near Fort Washita. A gentle and kindly man, he was well received by the Chickasaws and won many converts to his faith.

The most significant impact of the Methodists, however, was in the realm of education. Following removal tribal leaders had been slow to see the necessity of re-establishing some kind of educational system. Prodded by the Methodists, in 1844 the Chickasaws appropriated $12,000 from their national funds for the construction of the Chickasaw Manual Labor Academy. The institution opened in 1851 as a boarding school with sixty students and Reverend J. C. Robinson as superintendent. Coeducational, the academy offered instruction not only in basic academic disciplines but also in agricultural and mechanical arts as well as in "house-wifery." After 1854 the Methodists also contracted to operate Bloomfield Academy for girls and Colbert Institute for both boys and girls. Imitating the example of their religious competitors, the Presbyterians consented to administer two other Chickasaw academies: Wapanucka Institute for girls (1852) and Burney Institute for girls (1859).

In addition to these five national institutions, the Chickasaws illustrated their growing enthusiasm for education in other ways. In the 1850's they established a system of elementary neighborhood schools which were operational during the day and free to tribal youngsters. Six such schools with an enrollment of 180 students were reported at the first of the decade. Furthermore, the Chickasaws used part of their national funds to finance an advanced education for promising scholars in the states. Some of the young men so favored enrolled initially in the famous Choctaw Academy in Blue Springs, Kentucky; at a later time others enrolled in Plainfield Academy in Norwich, Connecticut, and Delaware College in Newark, Delaware.

While the Chickasaws were reconstructing the economic and social fabric of their nation, they were successfully constructing a viable political and governmental system. The 1837 Treaty of Doaksville had given the Chickasaws citizenship in the Choctaw Nation, the prerogative of indiscriminate settlement, and the right to form

"CIVILIZED CHICKASAW INDIANS" in the latter 19th Century.

a political district. The following year the Choctaws amended their constitution to accommodate the new arrivals, authorizing them to select one of four district chiefs and ten members of a forty member council. Concerned with more immediate problems, the Chickasaws did not participate in the government established until 1841 when they elected Isaac Alberson as District Chief and their quota of representatives.

Chief Alberson's authority, however, was not unchallenged. As a vestige of the past, King Ishtehotopa pretended to power, as did the Chickasaw Commission appointed to oversee tribal property interests prior to removal. Who would ultimately speak for the tribe was not determined until July, 1845. On the occasion of a national gathering near Boiling Springs, Pittman Colbert, a prominent mixed blood, made a play to restore all governmental authority to the king, including the right to control and distribute the tribal annuity. Though the plan was approved by a "rump" council, the federal government thwarted it by delivering the $70,000 annuity to Alberson. The decision increased the district chief's prestige, destroyed the power of the king and commission, and had the effect — beneficial from the point of view of the United States — of encouraging Chickasaw settlement in the assigned district. As a resident, Alberson paid the annuity at his home.

As more and more Chickasaws moved from the emigrant camps to be near the annuity payment, a healthy nationalism developed. Rather than be simply an appendage to the Choctaw Nation, tribal leaders determined to organize a government that would function separately. Accordingly, in 1848 they drafted a constitution that provided for a thirty member district council and an executive selected by the council. Edmund Pickens was chosen as the first chief. The child of nationalism, the new government did not disappoint those who served as mid-wives. Indeed, it became a vehicle in the renaissance of Chickasaw national life. Elected officials now argued that the tribe should have an independent political existence. When the Choctaws refused to accommodate them, the Chickasaws turned to the United States to effectuate independence. To federal officials they complained that the Choctaws treated them as intruders, refused to recognize their "ownership" of the tribal district, failed to acknowledge proper boundaries, and sought to control the tribe's trust funds. Justice, the Chickasaw leaders concluded, demanded a political divorce.

The campaign for independence proved successful. Having been persuaded by Chickasaw rhetoric, the United States ultimately forced the Choctaws to sign the Treaty of 1855. Negotiated in Washington, the agreement authorized the creation of an independent and sovereign Chickasaw Nation with boundaries encompassing the central portion of the original Choctaw domain. For a clear title to the region, the Chickasaws agreed to pay $150,000. That territory west of the tribal domain would be held in common by the two tribes but leased to the United States for $800,000 as a reserve for Plains Indians. The lease money would be divided at a ratio of three to one — the approximate population ratio — with the Choctaws receiving $600,000 and the Chickasaws $200,000.

To consumate their political rebirth, in August, 1856, the Chickasaws met near Tishomingo to adopt a new constitution. Jackson Kemp served as president of the convention, and Holmes Colbert and Sampson Folsom drafted the document. As written the constitution called for executive, legislative, and judicial departments. The executive, styled the "Governor of the Chickasaw Nation," and members of a bicameral legislature were to be elected by popular vote, while judges of the Supreme Court would be selected by the legislature. The document was promptly ratified, and several weeks later the first elections were held. Casting a vote by standing in line behind the candidate of their choice, the Chickasaws elected Cyrus Harris as their first governor and members of both legislative houses. When the new government assembled at the capitol building in

THE CHICKASAW NATION'S NATIONAL CAPITOL BUILDING at Tishomino, Indian Territory, erected after the political re-unification of the Chickasaws in 1856.

Tishomingo, the Chickasaws could properly celebrate their re-birth as an independent people.

Just how independent the tribe considered itself became apparent in 1861. When the southern states began to withdraw from the Union, the Chickasaws declared their intention of joining the Confederacy. Several factors motivated them in this course of action. Like the seceeding states, the Chickasaws were a slave-holding people. Moreover, their esteemed agent, Douglas Cooper, was an active southern sympathizer, and he, like citizens in Texas and Arkansas, carried on vigorous propaganda among them. Finally, in May, 1861, the United States abandoned Forts Washita and Arbuckle and left the Chickasaws to face southern pressures alone. No wonder that on May 25, 1861, the tribe declared its independence from the Washington government and on July 12 entered into a formal alliance with the Confederacy at North Fork Village in the Creek Nation!

In the war that followed, the Chickasaws played only a minor role. Commanded by Douglas Cooper, their men were organized into at least four regiments and given the assignment of patrolling the Arkansas-Canadian River line. Yet the Chickasaw troops ocassionally sallied out to do battle with Union forces. In November and December, 1861, they assisted in the maneuvers that forced the neutral Indians to retreat to Kansas. In March of the following year they helped cover the retreat of Confederate forces defeated at Pea Ridge, Arkansas, and then in the late summer of 1863 attempted to thwart Union occupation of Fort Smith. In 1864, the Chickasaws were unable to check a federal cavalry thrust that pushed to Fort Arbuckle, though they did contribute substantially to the Confederate victory at Poison Springs, Arkansas.

More important than the Chickasaw military effort were the social and economic dislocations that accompanied the war. After 1862 the tribal domain became the haven for Confederate exiles fleeing federal troops that occupied northern Indian Territory. The Chickasaws exerted every effort to feed the refugees but resources being limited such a task was impossible. The exiles formed marauding bands and took what was not given. The war, therefore, not only fostered an era of lawlessness but stymied economic development. It brought a halt as well to educational efforts and deterred any effective governmental operations. Indeed, all elements of national life were seriously disturbed.

The trauma of civil war ended finally in 1865. Though committed champions of southern rights, Chickasaw leaders recognized that defeat of Lee's army east of the Mississippi spelled the end of the Confederacy. Governor Winchester Colbert, therefore, signed terms of surrender on July 14, a point in time that gave the Chickasaws the distinction of being the last Confederate community to capitulate. The laying down of arms was formalized the following September at Fort Smith, Arkansas, when David Burney signed a simple treaty of peace and amnity with the federal commissioners.

A definitive peace settlement, though, was not concluded until April, 1866. Signed at Washington by the Chickasaws and Choctaws, the treaty was decidedly more favorable than those negotiated with other "rebel" tribes. The United States agreed to pay $300,000 to the two tribes for relinquishment of any title to the Leased District if they agreed to adopt their former slaves. If they refused, the money would be used to colonize the freedmen elsewhere. The treaty also authorized railroad right-of-way grants, called for allotment of land in severalty, and provided for an Indian Territory of Oklahoma. Finally, it directed the settlement of 10,000 Kansas Indians among the two tribes, authorized compensation of loyal Indians and traders, and established a United States court with limited jurisdiction in Indian Territory. For its part, the federal government promised to restore pre-1861 trust funds and to resume annuity payments. Given the punitive disposition of the Radical Republicans then in control of the U. S. Congress, these concessions were more liberal than the Chickasaws might have expected to receive. That they did suggested their diplomatic skill.

Once the tribe had ratified the Treaty of 1866, the Chickasaws turned their attention to the challenges of the postwar era. As defeated allies of the Confederacy, they were expected by the United States to demonstrate a submissive attitude and a measure of penance. Consequently, in 1867, the tribe wrote a new constitution which, though it retained the essential features of its predecessor, recognized the abolition of slavery. Yet the Chickasaws did not provide for the adoption of the freedmen as encouraged by the 1866 agreement. Indeed, throughout the remainder of their national existence, despite the importunities of the federal government, they steadfastly refused to adopt their ex-slaves. The tribe was more submissive, though, in its treatment of those 250 Chickasaws who had remained loyal to the United States during the Civil War. With only minor protests it permitted federal officials to compensate them from national funds.

Their penance completed, the Chickasaws directed their energies toward the social and economic rehabilitation of their nation. From the annuity distributed in 1867 the tribe appropriated funds sufficient to re-establish its educational system. Within four years enough neighborhood schools were in operation to provide instruction for 452 students. Not until 1876, however, did the Chickasaws re-open their boarding schools — Chickasaw Male Academy, Bloomfield, Wapanucka, and Lebanon Orphan School (previously Burney Institute). All tribal schools in the postwar era were initially operated by secular contractors who agreed to provide instruction and board for a pre-determined sum. Though the quality of education offered was open to suspicion, the tribe took pride in Chickasaw teachers instructing Chickasaw students. So enthusiastic were they that they normally invested as much as three-fourths of their annuity in education which on a per capita basis was more than any other Indian nation. An immediate dividend of the investment was a literacy rate of 50 per cent by 1880.

Like education, religious activity had been severely impeded by the Civil War. In the post-bellum period the missionaries redoubled efforts to win the Chickasaws from the lingering influence of *Ababinili.* Though the Methodists continued to be the most active, the Baptists, led by the indominitable Joseph S. Murrow, also engaged in a vigorous evangelical effort. The Cumberland Presbyterians soon resumed their work, as did the Roman Catholics. Despite the best efforts of the missionaries, the Chickasaws were not easily converted. In 1876, the government agent reported only 500 church members and ten church buildings. Still, the men of God believed that the Chickasaw field was "white unto harvest" if only the "reapers fainted not." After 1880 they won permission from the nation to underpin their evangelical work with an educational program. The Catholics established schools at Tishomingo and Purcell, and the Methodists opened Pierce Institute at White Bead Hill and Hargrove College at Ardmore. Such ventures aided the Christian cause, yet on the whole the tribe remained inured to the gospel call.

If the Chickasaws shunned the preachers, they had no reservation about listening to the apostles of capitalism. As in the United States, the postwar period in Indian Territory was an era of vital economic expansion. So vigorous was the development that if the tribe had been marked by the recent military conflict, it was soon indistinguishable. The coming of the railroad heralded the new era. The Missouri, Kansas and Texas (Katy) line, the beneficiary of a provision in the Treaty of 1866, built across the southeast corner of the Chickasaw Nation in 1872. The Santa Fe laid track south from Purcell, reaching Texas in 1887. Five other lines, including the Rock Island and the Frisco, also constructed roads through the nation.

The completion of the railroad network stimulated other economic activity. With international markets accessible, the Chickasaws opened new fields to plant wheat, corn, and oats. Indeed, the Washita Valley became a "solid farm for 50 miles." Between 1875 and 1887 agricultural production nearly doubled, reaching 25,000 bushels of wheat, 125,000 bushels of corn, and 30,000 bushels of oats. The expansion of cotton culture was just as dramatic. Ardmore received and shipped 60,000 bales cotton annually. In addition to agriculture, the railroads also stimulated quarrying and lumbering.

Though not directly connected with railroad activity, ranching was another important aspect of the Chickasaw economic boom. The vast prairies in the western portion of the nation provided terrain and grass sufficient to sustain a veritable cattle empire. Herds of Texas cattle lingered in the region gaining weight before they trailed further north to Abilene. Made aware of this resource, many Chickasaws built their own herds and took advantage of the profitable markets. In 1882 government agents reported that as many as 140,000 head of cattle and a substantial number of horses and sheep belonged to Indian owners. Even more cattle were owned by Texans who established ranches such as the Hook Nine on tribal lands leased from co-operative Chickasaws.

The development of the economic resources of the tribe increased the treasury and brought a measure of prosperity shared by most citizens. From federally invested funds amounting to $1,167,667, the nation annually received more than $65,000. This sum was supplemented by royalties received from the exploitation of natural resources. Non-Indian cattlemen paid yearly an assessment of twenty-five cents per head grazed, while lumbermen were charged $5.00 for each 1,000 board feet exported. As these resources were held in common with the Choctaws as per the Treaty of 1837, the Chickasaws shared the royalties received with them on the ratio of three to one. Likewise, the Choctaws divided royalties received from coal mining — $79,146 in 1897 — on the same basis. The tribe, however, did not divide receipts derived from permits purchased by non-Indians living in the Chickasaw Nation. Payable annually, the permit charge ranged from twenty-five cents in 1871 to $25 in 1876 to $5 in 1880. Money paid into the treasury, of course, went for national purposes, enabling all Chickasaws to share in the benefits. Yet the general prosperity enriched many citizens individually, furthering the tribe's reputation of being most blessed financially.

Yet the economic revolution was not always positive in its impact. For one thing, the Chickasaw Nation with a relative constant Indian population of 6,000 was inundated by white men. Within ten years of the Civil War the whites numbered more than 4,500. This compares with 800 among the Cherokees, 400 among the Creeks, and 200 among the

Choctaws. During the 1870's Governor B. F. Overton tried to stem the settler tide by raising the permit fee to $25 annually, but to no avail. By 1893 more than 40,000 non-Indians occupied the tribal domain. In time such a large alien population changed the character of society in the Chickasaw Nation. Once rural in orientation, social activity came to focus upon bustling urban centers such as Ardmore, Chickasha, Purcell, Ada, Pauls Valley, and Tishomingo. That white residents of these communities had no title to the land made little difference. They acted as if they were permanent citizens, ignored and segregated the out-numbered Indians, and refused to be bound by Chickasaw law. So blatant was the civil disobedience of white residents of Pickens County that tribal leaders referred to the area as the "Free State of Pickens."

Criminal lawlessness was another legacy of the white innundation. Despite tribal and federal statutes to the contrary, whiskey was imported into the Chickasaw Nation with apparent impunity. Under the influence of alcohol, some normally law abiding Indians went on drunken rampages that frequently resulted in destruction and death. In 1883 alone, eleven murders perpetrated by Chickasaws were recorded. Moreover the guilty were generally beyond the reach of tribal and United States courts. Reasonably sure that crimes would go unpunished if

64

NELSON CHIGLEY, President of the Chickasaw Senate, who once served as Governor for a few days.

not actually undetected, many non-Indians made the Chickasaw domain a theater for robbery, cattle rustling, and murder. Though tribal officials realized that such activity eroded public confidence in their ability to govern, they could do little to correct the situation.

Lawlessness was only a minor aspect of the larger problem confronting the Chickasaw leaders. Much more basic was how to deal with the total impact of the social and economic changes occuring in the postwar era. Many Chickasaws, especially the mixed-bloods, welcomed the transformations and hoped to facilitate them. Other leaders, primarily full-bloods, abhored the alterations in traditional society and worked actively to restore the ancient ways. To espouse these different views, the Chickasaws formed two loosely organized political parties, the Progressive and the Pullback. Leaders of these parties who attained public office were generally capable and qualified and met annually at the capitol building in Tishomingo to transact national business. Governors who served the tribe in the postbellum era, most of whom were Pullbacks, distinguished themselves in their patriotism and dedication. These included Cyrus Harris, B. F. Overton, Jonas Wolf, William M. Guy, William L. Byrd, Palmer S. Mosley, and Douglas H. Johnston.

Chickasaw public life was seldom serene. As white induced changes multiplied, tribal elections were highly acrimonious and their results usually disputed. One such contest occurred in 1888. Two years previously the Progressive candidate, William M. Guy, had defeated the Pullback nominee, William L. Byrd, by one vote. Governor Guy used his term to facilitate the progressive cause, permitting the Santa Fe railroad to lay track through the Chickasaw Nation. Incensed by this accommodation, Byrd challenged the incumbent's bid for re-election. The returns showed Guy the victor, but the legislature after a successful Pullback challenge of some ballots declared Byrd the new governor. At that point Guy's supporters marched upon the capitol and induced the legislature to retract its verdict. Biding their time, the Pullbacks waited until the Progressives left Tishomingo, whereupon they returned to the capitol and installed Byrd as the chief executive. Further conflict was avoided only when United States officials acted to sustain the Pullbacks in the action taken.

Though domestic change and political activity occupied much of the tribe's attention, the Chickasaws were always vigilant in their intercourse with the United States. Such watchfulness had as its objective the preservation and implementation of all rights pledged in earlier treaties. Detecting federal mis-management of their trust fund, in 1887 they won a decision from the United States Court of Claims that directed the government to restore some

$240,164 to the fund. Cooperating with the Choctaws, the Chickasaws also gained a measure of compensation for the Leased District. As understood by the tribes, they had ceded the district in 1855 for the settlement of Plains Indians. In 1891 when the government opened up a part of the area to white settlement, Congress recognized such an interpretation and appropriated $2,991,405 to quiet the joint title to those lands not administered as promised. Divided by the usual three to one ratio, in 1893, the Chickasaws distributed their portion in per capita payments. The tribe also shared with the Choctaws a $68,102 award ordered by the United States Supreme Court as compensation for the erroneously surveyed Arkansas boundary.

Of principal concern to the Chickasaws in their relationship with the United States, however, was the retention of their political independence and sovereignty. This task proved to be arduous and frustrating, for pressure to dissolve the governments of the Indian nations and to open their domain to white settlement intensified with each passing year. The Treaty of 1866 had called for a territorial government that would prepare the tribes for eventual statehood. Pressed by the United States to implement the plan, the Chickasaws met with other Indians in 1870 at Okmulgee in the Creek Nation to write a constitution providing for the political unification of the tribes. The resulting document was never ratified, primarily because the Chickasaws and other smaller tribes objected to the lack of equal representation for all Indian groups in at least one of the legislative bodies. The Okmulgee Council, however, with Chickasaw representatives present continued to meet informally until 1876, providing the tribes with a public forum to oppose federal schemes and legislation designed to subvert treaty provisions and to terminate tribal independence.

The interest of the United States in territorial status for the Indians was simply a means of opening tribal lands for white exploitation. When the tribes rejected the subterfuge, Washington officials then turned another. In the 1880's they adopted the view that civilization of the Indians could be furthered only if their communal system of property ownership were terminated, if they were settled on individual homesteads, and if they were surrounded by exemplary white farmers. For a time the Chickasaws and other Civilized Tribes successfully combatted implementation of this policy, but the greed of the white man was so insatiable that the Indians could not permanently resist. Ultimately, on March 3, 1893, Congress created the so-called Dawes Commission and authorized it to enter into negotiations with the Chickasaws and sister tribes to terminate tribal government and allot Indian lands.

In its initial discussions with the Civilized Tribes, the commission found them wholly uncooperative. It reported the attitude to Washington. Congress responded by authorizing a careful survey of all Indian lands and preparation of tribal rolls. Believing that further resistance was foolish, Choctaw leaders negotiated an agreement at Muskogee in December, 1896, whereby they agreed to an allotment of the combined Choctaw and Chickasaw domain among enrolled citizens of the two tribes. Chickasaw Governor Palmer Mosley, however, objected to this unilateral and preemptory action. Dispatching a delegation to Washington to protest the agreement, he succeeded in preventing final congressional approval.

The government, though, did not abandon its goal of alloting the Chickasaw domain. Aware of this and fearful that allotment might be imposed from above, Chickasaw officials reluctantly agreed to negotiate. Meeting in Atoka in April, 1897, they joined Choctaw leaders in accepting a compact that provided for allotment of the tribal domain and termination of their national governments. The agreement also directed that townsites be reserved from allotment and sold separately, the proceeds of which would be paid per capita to citizens by blood; that mineral reserves be used for public benefit; and that trust funds held by the United States be capitalized and paid out per capita. It further

70

AH-IT-TO-TUBBY, Chickasaw councilor and delegate to Washington during America's "Gilded Age." This photograph was made around 1875.

specified that Choctaw freedmen should receive forty acre allotments, that title to all allotments should be inalienable and non-taxable for twenty-five years and that tribal government should cease March 4, 1906, when the Indians would become citizens of the United States.

Despite the concurrance of tribal leaders in the Atoka Agreement, the Chickasaws as a whole were still reluctant to confirm their national demise. Indeed, in an election held in December, 1897, the allotment compact was rejected. Congress responded by passing the Curtis Act, essentially an Organic Act for Indian Territory, which directed that the Agreement should be submitted again for tribal consideration and, moreover, that the Chickasaws should be compelled to provide forty acre allotments for their still unadopted freedmen. As procastination seemed only to elicit harsher demands, the Chickasaws accepted the inevitable and voted with the Choctaws to approve tribal liquidation.

With allotment approved, the Dawes Commission proceeded to establish a roll according to which land could be distributed. It proved to be a difficult task. Hoping to take advantage of any property settlement, many unqualified individuals improperly declared that they too were Chickasaws. Though most such applicants were rejected by the commission, federal courts admitted 1,000's to citizenship. Moreover, federal officials were required to admit to the roll more than 4,000 freedmen, despite the fact that the Chickasaws had never owned more than 1,000 slaves or agreed to adopt them. In order to protect their inheritance, tribal leaders employed the McAlester law firm of Mansfield, McMurray, and Cornish. In 1902, these attorneys assisted the tribe in negotiating a Supplemental Agreement to the Atoka accord which set out detailed allotment procedures and provided for the sale of mineral lands within three years. More importantly, it created a citizenship court to rule on disputed applications and authorized the Chickasaws to litigate before the United States Court of Claims the question of freedmen participation in the tribal estate.

The implementation of the Supplemental Agreement required the joint endorsement of the Chickasaws and the Choctaws. Whether or not to ratify the measure became the central issue in the tribal election 1902. The Pullback candidate, William L. Byrd, opposed the agreement, while the Progressive nominee, Palmer Mosley, supported it. Mosley won the governorship, but only because the Chickasaw legislature threw out the votes of Pontotoc County, a Pullback stronghold. Armed retaliation was narrowly averted by the timely arrival of United States officials. Mosley then joined with Douglas H. Johnston and Ben Colbert in a campaign that won ratification of the Supplemental Agreement.

In one sense, the adoption of the agreement proved most beneficial. The Citizenship Court authorized by the measure allowed only 156 of the 3,403 applications for admission to the Chickasaw and Choctaw rolls. Moreover, their attorneys successfully argued in the courts that unadopted Chickasaw freedmen were not entitled to share in the tribal estate. In 1910, Congress appropriated $606,936 as compensation for this error. Given these successful challenges, the roll as finally established enumerated 1,538 fullblood Chickasaws, 4,146 mixed bloods, 635 intermarried whites, and 4,670 Negroes.

With the tribe enrolled, the Dawes Commission proceeded with allotment. During 1899 and 1900 field parties had surveyed the 4,707,904 acres of the Chickasaw Nation, rated each forty acre tract according to physical features, and assigned to each tract an arbitrary monetary value. Entitled to 320 acres of average land evaluated at $1,040.28, each Chickasaw could select as little as 160 acres of choice bottom land or as much as 4,165 acres of less desirable terrain. Furthermore, he could select his land in compact or widely scattered tracts. In offices at Tishomingo and Atoka allotments began in 1903 and continued for a decade.

As each Chickasaw and Choctaw was entitled

MEMBERS OF THE LAST CHICKASAW LEGISLATURE in 1906. The arrow identifies Governor Douglas H. Johnston.

to only 320 acres of average land, some three million acres of their combined domain remained unallotted. These lands included 444,052 acres of coal and asphalt reserves, a large tract of timber land, and tracts for some ninety different towns. The dissolution agreements had directed that this part of the estate be sold and that proceeds be paid per capita to the tribes. Sale of town lots and timber lands eventually netted more than $3 million and enabled per capita payments in 1904, 1906 and 1908. Because of a nationwide depression, leases, and government red tape, the segregated coal and asphalt lands were not sold until well after the tribal period.

As the dissolution agreements had stipulated the cessation of tribal government in March, 1906, Chickasaw national leaders exercised only limited authority until that time. The legislature could enact no laws without the approval of the President of the United States, tribal schools passed to the control of the federal government, and issues of law were transferred to United States Courts. Douglas H. Johnston served as the last governor, although he was continued in that office at the pleasure of the President after 1907.

When Chickasaw leaders came to recognize the inevitability of their national demise, they demonstrated little concern as to the procedure which would finalize the process. When other

Indian leaders acted to prevent Indian Territory from being made a part of Oklahoma Territory, Governor Johnston refused to participate. Therefore, in August, 1905, the Chickasaws were only observers of the movement to form the separate Indian state of Sequoyah, though Johnston did send "Alfalfa Bill" Murray, an intermarried Chickasaw and later governor of Oklahoma, as his representative. It was just as well, for congress had already decided to unite Oklahoma and Indian Territories into a single governmental entity. Accordingly, in June, 1906, it passed the Oklahoma Enabling Act authorizing a constitutional convention that met the following November in Guthrie. Bill Murray was elected president of the body and materially shaped the constitution ultimately adopted by the voters of both territories. Oklahoma entered the Union on November 16, 1907, and with its admission the Chickasaw Nation existed only in the minds and hearts of a still proud people.

INTO THE TWENTIETH CENTURY

Many sincere friends of the Indians believed that termination and land allotment would prove beneficial to the first Americans. Others were just as convinced that it would bring despair, poverty, and human disintegration. Referring to the impact upon the Indian of the admission of Oklahoma into the Union, the popular Baptist missionary to the Chickasaws,

78

J. F. Murrow, predicted, "I think inside of a year that the full-bloods [will] be deprived of almost every bit of their property." Unfortunately, Murrow proved more right than wrong. In a veritable orgy of plunder, the Chickasaws lost much of their inheritance. Shrewd and immoral "grafters" used a variety of techniques to accomplish this end. After winning the confidence of unsuspecting Indians, they induced them to enter allotments far distant from their homes and then leased the land for a mere pittance of its value. Others secured powers of attorney and used the land to their own benefit. Some had themselves named beneficiaries of wills and then inherited the land after the allottee "disappeared." Still others secured court appointments as guardians of incompetents and minors and then administered the estate in such a way as to enrich themselves.

Of all the methods conceived to divest the Indian of his land, the most successful had the full consent of Congress and the state of Oklahoma. In 1904 federal legislation enabled enrolled adult whites and Negroes to sell all but their 160 acre homestead, a measure that opened some 299,000 Chickasaw acres to white purchase. Pressed by an Oklahoma delegation that included Congressmen Charles Carter, an enrolled Chickasaw, in 1908 Congress removed all restrictions on whites, blacks, and mixed-bloods of less than one-half Indian blood, permitting them to sell their entire 320 acre allotment. Chickasaws of more than one-half but less than three-fourths Indian blood were enabled to market all but their 160 acre homestead, while restrictions on those of more than three-fourths Indian blood were continued. The general effect of this law was to stimulate a spree of land buying, exploitation and dispossession. Made aware of this unfortunate circumstance by such organizations as the Indian Rights Association, in 1928 and again in 1932 Congress acted to continue restrictions on the fullbloods and to reimpose them upon halfbloods until 1953. Yet the damage had been done; the precious inheritance of most Chickasaws had been wasted.

As individual Indians were losing their allotments, tribal and Choctaw leaders pressed the government to dispose of those 3,000,000 acres withheld from general allotment. These lands, of course, included townsites, timber lands, and coal and asphalt reserves. Initiated during the tribal period, the sale of town lots was concluded by 1915. Most of the timber land was sold between 1914 and 1916, but the Chickasaws and Choctaws experienced constant frustration in the liquidation of the mineral resources. Providing as much as $250,000 annually in royalties, this valuable tract was withheld from sale by the government due to existing leases and bureaucratic indifference.

CHICKASAWS AND CHOCTAWS receiving payments from sale of their tribal patrimony from officials of the U.S. Bureau of Indian Affairs in September, 1908.

Wholly suspicious of government control, the tribes insisted that the lands be sold according to the dissolution agreements. Finally, by 1918 all surface rights and 64,415 acres of sub-surface rights were successfully marketed, the revenue from which brought the total amount produced from all sales between 1910 and 1919 to $19,775,436.

The dissolution agreements had provided that proceeds derived from the unallotted lands should be paid per capita to enrolled citizens. Before such payments occurred, however, the Chickasaws and Choctaws had to engage in a bitter struggle to preserve the integrity of their rolls. Now that citizenship had a tangible quantity, many who had been denied admission to the rolls by the Citizenship Court reasserted their "rights." Choctaws still resident in Mississippi also demanded to participate in the division of the jointly held estate. Such attempts, fortunately, were thwarted by a watchful leadership and a vigilant Oklahoma congressional delegation. Accordingly, payments to enrolled Chickasaws or their heirs began in 1916 and extended to 1925. Including earlier allocations from town lot sales and liquidation of trust funds, per capita shares equalled $1,075.

Save for the sale of 444,052 acres of coal and asphalt reserves, by 1929 the tribal estate was largely liquidated. With their inheritance, collectively as well as individually, nearly wasted, it is surprising that the Chickasaws were able to retain a measure of group identity. This resulted primarily from the continuation of tribal government, if only in ill-defined form. Retained in office at the pleasure of the President, D. H. Johnston served as governor of the Chickasaw people until his death in 1939. Though an advocate of assimilation through removal of restrictions and speedy sale of the tribal estate, he nonetheless functioned as a symbol of the past, preventing total destruction of all things Chickasaw. Johnston was succeeded by Floyd E. Maytubby. Upon Maytubby's death in 1963, Overton James was appointed as Governor of the Chickasaw Nation.

The youngest ever to serve as governor and of five-eights Indian blood, James has provided brilliant leadership. Though an informal advisory council existed in earlier days, James has established a nine member council with which he advises on a regular basis. Moreover, James established local councils in six different counties and has directed that the tribe as a whole congregate annually at Byng, Oklahoma. He has also continued Chickasaw participation in the Inter-Tribal Council of the Five Civilized Tribes, of which he has served as president for four terms. The Chickasaws have so welcomed his leadership that in 1971 when he stood for election against four opponents, he received 85 per cent of the votes cast. On the basis of this mandate, Governor James has recently taken steps that will provide the Chickasaws with a written constitution and a well-defined governmental organization.

Though of limited authority, tribal leadership especially during recent years has proved most beneficial to the Chickasaw people. A conspicuous success has been in the area of federal relations. Working with Choctaw leaders and the Oklahoma congressional delegation, the Chickasaws and Choctaws finally gained the approval of Congress whereby the United States would purchase the residue of the coal and asphalt lands for $8,500,000. The transaction permitted a per capita payment of more than $300 in 1949.

Assisted by able attorneys, the tribe has also initiated litigation in the United States Court of Claims and before the Indian Claims Commission seeking adjustments of long-standing disputes with the government. Decisions by the later tribunal in 1950 awarded the Chickasaws and Choctaws $3,489,843 as additional compensation for their coal and asphalt lands. This judgment enabled yet another substantial per capita payment in 1953. A 1972 decision of the United States Supreme Court, though, has provided the most fitting culmination to these legal efforts. The Court declared that title to the bed of the Arkansas River had not passed to Oklahoma upon statehood but had been retained by

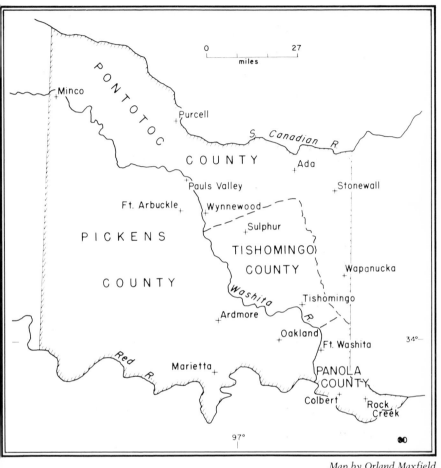

MAP 3. The Chickasaw Nation territory and its subdivisions about 1890.

the original Indian owners. Therefore, royalties accruing to the state from sand, gravel, and oil leases since 1907 should have been paid to the initial possessors. Whether the Chickasaws and Choctaws hold an undisputed title to the river bed between the mouth of the Canadian and Fort Smith or share ownership with the Cherokees remains to be adjudicated. Whatever the legal determination to that question, the two tribes stand to gain millions of dollars in back and future royalties.

Tribal leadership has continued to emphasize the importance of education. Though most Chickasaw youngsters attend public schools in Oklahoma, some take advantage of educational opportunities offered at Carter Seminary in Ardmore as well as other Indian boarding schools. Notably, some 80 per cent of those graduating from high school today seek higher education at any one of the colleges and universities throughout Oklahoma. This remarkable interest in post-high school work is encouraged by the tribe, which provides a $100 clothing grant for youngsters of one-fourth Chickasaw blood. An adult education program at Murray State College in Tishomingo also receives the endorsement of the tribe. Governor James himself personifies the tribal committment to education. Holding the B. A. and M. A. degrees from Southeastern State College in Durant, he serves today as the Director of

Indian Education for all of Oklahoma.

The zeal with which the Chickasaws pursue education stems in large part from their desire to share fully in the economic benefits of modern America. Since the dissolution of the tribal estate, many Chickasaws, particularly the mixed-bloods, have successfully negotiated the intricacies of an economic system that is acquisitive and competitive in character. Some of these, because of the discovery of oil on their restricted allotments, have become wealthy. Yet others, especially those of more than one-half Indian blood, have been less adroit and have been reduced to various stages of poverty. Tribal leaders have not been unmindful of these unfortunate Chickasaws. Indeed, it is in this area that the most noteable advances have been made. Headed by Leland Keel, the Chickasaw Housing Authority has assumed responsibility for providing 300 leased homes and constructing 770 mutual help homes and 562 low-rent units. All leased homes and a majority of the mutual-help homes are for the use of qualified Chickasaws, a significant step in Governor James' goal of having all of his people in modern homes by 1976.

The tribe has sponsored and encouraged other programs designed to improve the economic status of its citizens. Arts and craft centers have been established at Tishomingo and Ardmore to provide training and commercial outlets for those with native skills. The Neighborhood Youth Corp has enabled many young Chickasaws to find gainful employment, as has an energetic job placement office. The Adult Vocational Training Program sponsored by the Bureau of Indian Affairs offers many adults an opportunity to better themselves economically through vocational education. Probably the most remarkable economic development in recent years, however, has been the tribal purchase of a seventy-two unit motel in Sulphur, Oklahoma. Renamed the "Chickasaw Motor Inn," the enterprise has provided employment for several tribal members, is a symbol of Indian economic vitality, and returns profits to the general operating fund of the nation.

As Governor James and his Advisory Council work to achieve economic viability for the Chickasaws, they endeavor simultaneously to advance the tribe socially. Once totally dependent for health services upon the Indian hospital at distant Talihina, the Chickasaws have secured the establishment of a clinic at Tishomingo and the designation of Ada as a site for a $10 million hospital. A community health program headed by the gracious and capable Geraldine Greenwood provides family planning assistance, general public health services, friendly counseling, and attentative listeners.

Though the Chickasaws live in a predominately white society, tribal leaders have

CHICKASAW NATION GOVERNOR OVERTON JAMES concluding the transaction by which the Chickasaw Nation purchased the Chickasaw Motor Inn in September of 1972.

worked to preserve what remains of their cultural integrity. The annual meeting at Byng, the Chickasaw language classes, and the arts and crafts programs all testify to this effort. Governor James has also begun quarterly publication of *The Chickasaw Newsletter* which keeps the Chickasaws abreast of tribal activity. He has also sought — unsuccessfully thus far — to reacquire the old tribal capitol building at Tishomingo, now the courthouse of Johnston County. An adjacent building which encloses a replica of the first Chickasaw council house, though, has been erected by the Oklahoma Historical Society. More importantly, in early 1973 the nation brought out the *Chickasaw Dictionary,* thanks to the prayerful efforts of the late Jesse Humes and Vinnie May Humes, the step-father and mother of Governor James. Giving English words and the Chickasaw equivalent, the work is designed to remind young Chickasaws of their proud heritage. Mrs. Hume is presently supplementing this monumental effort by recording on tape the proper pronunciation of many words listed.

Yet the effort to preserve the rich Chickasaw heritage has proved a difficult task. Never large, the tribe after the Civil War so intermarried with the more predominate whites that by 1906 more than one-half of its number had less than one-fourth Indian blood. Today the 8,000 Chickasaws are more completely intermarried

Photograph by W. David Baird

MISS GEORGIA BROWN, Chickasaw Princess for 1973. Elected annually, the Chickasaw Princess represents her tribe at local, state, and regional ceremonies, where she
epitomizes Chickasaw beauty, grace and manners.

than any of the Five Civilized Tribes. As a consequence, no more than 300 to 500 are full bloods. This biologic assimilation tends to encourage large-scale cultural assimilation and unawareness of the proud story of the Chickasaw people.

THE FUTURE

As a small minority in a non-Indian world will the Chickasaws survive into the 21st Century? One needs only to visit with Governor James at the state capitol, with Mrs. Greenwood in Ada, with Georgia Brown, the Chickasaw Princess, in Tishomingo, or O. J. Parnell, the manager of the Chickasaw Inn, in Sulphur to know that they will Indeed, one is convinced that the current economic, social, and cultural renaissance will insure the Chickasaws of not only a future existence but a productive and meaningful life. Let us, however, be more specific.

With regard to population, the number of those who classify themselves as Chickasaws will increase in the years to come. To be sure the amount of Indian blood will be diluted, but that will not represent a disappearance of the Chickasaw strain so much as a widening of its influence. Though the focus of population will remain in southcentral Oklahoma, the future undoubtedly will witness a dispersion to urban centers across the United States. Yet wherever the Chickasaws live they will accomplish a complete integration of the predominately non-Indian society.

Several factors lend credence to this conclusion. With a long tradition of educational excellence, Chickasaw youngsters will have academic training sufficient to permit them to compete with any American. Furthermore, tribal commitment to vocational instruction will insure adults an equal opportunity to secure whatever jobs are available. At this point, though, a note of caution is necessary. If well-trained and skilled Chickasaws are to be fully employed, a continual and tireless effort to locate small industries near their residences is absolutely necessary. Governor Overton James is working to this end, and given his record in other fields, should be successful. Knowing that the Chickasaws will be benefited, James also hopes to stimulate an active tourist trade. The Chickasaw Motor Inn and the renaming of Platt National Park located at Sulphur to Chickasaw National Recreation Area are only two examples of how he hopes to capitalize upon this opportunity.

In their quest for a meaningful and productive life, the Chickasaws will not be detained by sub-standard housing or dehabilitating disease. No doubt Governor James will meet his pledge to provide modern housing for all of his people. New hospital facilities and continuation of the community health program will release the

94

Photograph by W. David Baird

MR. ABIJAH COLBERT, 75 years of age in 1973, a long time member of the Chickasaw Tribal Council.

Chickasaws from a preoccupation with the physical maintenance of life and enable them to seek instead a life of quality and refinement.

Though the Chickasaws will continue the economic and social integration of a non-Indian society, they will not forget that which makes them a distinctive and special people — a timeless heritage. Though once destined for oblivion that heritage is now being recalled and perpetuated. A formal constitution, annual meetings, arts and crafts, language preservation, place names, and tribal publications all testify to this renewed interest. Yet hopefully the Chickasaws can do more. Reacquisition of the old tribal capitol building, the creation of a culture center, and an active language instruction program would be positive steps. If the tribe is thwarted in these efforts, though, the current cultural renaissance will be sufficient to sustain the growing pride in all things Chickasaw. Knowledgeable of the past and skilled in the present, the Chickasaw people face the future with every prospect of achieving a rich and meaningful life. Though no longer "beloved warriors," they nonetheless remain "unconquered and unconquerable."

THE CHICKASAW MEDALLION

The design Indian Tribal Series employed for the obverse of its silver medallion for the Chickasaw Nation shows two breech-clout clad men working on a dug-out canoe. This came as something of a surprise to many people. The reason appears to be that after the United States forcibly removed the Chickasaw people from their aboriginal homeland with its huge rivers, most people forgot the crucial role canoes originally played in Chickasaw life.

The fact of the matter is that for hundreds of years, canoes provided the Chickasaws with indispensible mobility on the broad waters of the Mississippi, Ohio, Tennessee and tributary rivers. Felling giant cypress trees, Chickasaws burned and scraped out dug-out war canoes capable of carrying 60 or more warriors. Other native Americans from the middle Ohio to the Mississippi River Delta on the Gulf of Mexico lived in dread of the massive Chickasaw war canoes. Even though their population was never very large, the Chickasaws themselves held the

98

east bank of the mainstreams from above modern Louisville on the Ohio to below Memphis on the Mississippi.

Even after European colonial powers invaded North America, the Chickasaw war canoe remained a military factor to be reckoned with.

The Spanish explorer Fernando de Sota and his men were the first Europeans to repent their aggression against Chickasaws. After wintering in a Chickasaw town, de Sota demanded hundreds of Chickasaw bearers to help his expedition on its way. Rather than assume such a demeaning role, the Chickasaws burned the Spaniards out of their winter quarters. When the Spaniards crossed the Mississippi River to the west bank, perhaps 200 Chickasaw war canoes harried the crossing, according to the accounts of survivors interviewed by the Inca Garcilaso de la Vega and the anonymous Gentleman from Elvas.

A century and a half later, French colonials began exploring the Mississippi River as an avenue of rapid communication between settlements in Canada and Louisiana. The French colonial forces soon discovered the might of the Chickasaw war canoe to their everlasting regret.

The French colonists themselves gained a reputation as great canoe-men on the Great Lakes, the Mississippi River system, and other streams. Yet even the French rivermen could not breach the barrier of Chickasaw war canoes and shoreline marksmen when the Chickasaws determined to cut commerce on the Mississippi. After French colonial officials formed strategic alliances with tribes opposed to the Chickasaws, and undertook military campaigns against the latter, the Chickasaws blockaded the Mississippi against French river traffic.

In the early 1720's, the Chickasaws cut French river traffic on the Mississippi and sent their heavy cypress war canoes ranging widely up and down stream from their strongholds at the Chickasaw Bluffs on the east bank. They stopped the French rivermen for perhaps four years. The Europeans re-opened the Mississippi to their movements only by dint of building larger boats that could mount small cannon on swivels with which to bombard Chickasaw war canoes and keep them at a safe distance. Even then, the French rivermen sailed the Chickasaw stretch of the Mississippi in multiple-boat convoys that hugged the western shore of the river as far from Chickasaw marksmen and war canoe launching beaches as possible.

A decade later, when the French governor of Louisiana launched land assaults against the palisaded and moated Chickasaw towns, the Chickasaw war canoes surprised French munition boats on the Mississippi River. Capturing French powder, balls, and firearms intended to supply the amphibious assault forces, the Chickasaws turned the French munitions against the French and Indian allies. They cut to pieces the assault troops in withering cross-fire from bulwarks at the corners of their palisades — a supposedly European fortification defense tactic. The French governor had to retreat. Later, his King recalled him as a direct consequence of his defeat at the hands of Chickasaws.

The historic importance of the cypress war canoe in Chickasaw riverine military prowess is abundantly documented in the French colonial archives!

THE GREAT SEAL OF THE CHICKASAW NATION

After the Chickasaws separated politically from the Choctaws in 1856, they adopted their own seal. Reportedly, the manuscript copy of their new ordinances was lost on its way to the printer. New documents were adopted for the official seal in "Convention of Camp Harris" August 16, 1867. The official papers of Governor Cyrus Harris were using the seal in 1872.

The seal shows a Chickasaw warrior of ancient times standing erect, clad in moccasins, knee-wraps and breechcloth, with feathers in his hair. He holds two arrows in his right hand. He carries more arrows in a large quiver across his back. His left hand grasps his long hickory bow, while his defensive shield is tied to his left forearm.

SUGGESTED READINGS

Literature dealing with the entirety of the Chickasaw story is relatively scarce. In the main, the books listed below relate to different periods of tribal history and should be available in most major libraries. Shorter and more detailed studies may be found in several scholarly journals.

ADAIR, JAMES. *The History of the American Indians.* Reprint. New York: Johnson Reprint Corporation, 1968.

An excellent, first-hand account of the Chickasaws by an early English trader.

DEBO, ANGIE. *And Still The Waters Run.* Princeton: Princeton University Press, 1940.

A splendid study of the dissolution of tribal estates and the significance of that action for Oklahoma Indians during the 20th Century.

_____. *The Rise and Fall of the Choctaw Republic.* Norman: University of Oklahoma Press, 1934.

As the Choctaw story parallels that of the Chickasaws, this is an indispensable study.

CRANE, VERNER W. *The Southern Frontier, 1670 – 1732.* Ann Arbor: The University of Michigan Press, 1929.

A classic study on British ambitions in the

Mississippi Valley and how they influenced the Chickasaws.

GIBSON, ARREL M. *The Chickasaws.* Norman: University of Oklahoma Press, 1971.

The best general account of the Chickasaws, though it gives short shrift to the post-Civil War period and fails to deal with the 20th Century.

MALONE, JAMES H. *The Chickasaw Nation.* Louisville, Kentucky: John P. Martin and Company, 1922.

A short sketch of a noble people.

SWANTON, JOHN R. *Social and Religious Beliefs and Usages of the Chickasaw Indians* in *44th Annual Report of the Bureau of American Ethnology.* Washington: Government Printing Office, 1928.

A classic study of the ancient practices and views of the Chickasaws.

————. *The Indians of the Southeastern United States* in *Bureau of American Ethnology Bulletin No. 137.* Washington: Government Printing Office, 1946.
Contains a good deal of material on the early life ways of the southern Indians.

THE AUTHOR

W. DAVID BAIRD, who holds a Ph.D. degree from the University of Oklahoma, is an associate professor of History at the University of Arkansas. A native of Oklahoma, he has long been interested in the Indian tribes resident in that State. Baird is the author of *Peter Pitchlynn: Chief of the Choctaws* (University of Oklahoma Press, 1972), *The Osage People* (Indian Tribal Series, 1972), and *The Choctaw People* (Indian Tribal Series, 1973). He has also written a number of articles in professional journals on the American Indian. Assisted by a grant from the American Philosophical Society, his present research interest is the history of the Quapaw Indians.

104